NATIONAL GEOGRAPHIC

Ladders

THE DISAPPEARING BADLANDS

GULLIES, BUTTES, AND HOODOOS

by Robert Phalen

To visitors seeing it for the first time, Badlands National Park looks as forbidding as the moon. It's a barren, treeless land of cliffs and canyons, where summers are sizzling hot. Still, visitors feel a sense of wonder and curiosity.

Each year, thousands of visitors fill up their water bottles, put on their sunglasses, and head out into the park.

From the ridge called the Wall, the Badlands look impossible to cross without a path. A visitor can see why Native Americans called this place *mako sica*, meaning "land bad." In those days there were no roads or trails. People who wanted to cross this dangerous land had to find their own way through it. Modern trails have made hiking here much safer.

The Badlands are fringed by prairie grasslands, where herds of pronghorn sheep and bison graze.

TTES,

Visitors can follow one of these trails through the Wall and down into a deep, narrow canyon. Other canyons branch off and form a network of winding paths. Some canyons dead-end and some continue. In the deeper parts, tall cliffs create shade. Every visitor has probably wondered how this place could ever form.

Sediments such as clay particles, silt, and sand built up over tens of millions of years. As the sediments were deposited, they formed layers that hardened into rock.

Then 500,000 years ago, **weathering** and **erosion** began to carve the rock into the landscape you see today. Weathering is the wearing down of rock and soil. Erosion is the movement of rock and soil from one place to another.

In addition to the wild scenery, the Badlands also contain rich deposits of **fossils.** Protecting these fossils was one reason the area was made a national monument in 1929. In 1978, the Badlands became a national park.

READING THE ROCKS

The trail descends through canyons and comes out onto bare rock. In the sunlight, hikers squint at the landscape. It is striped with horizontal layers of **sedimentary rock.** Each layer of rock is a unique color, so the layers look like colorful spines in a stack of gigantic books.

Like books, the layers offer information that a trained eye can read. Each layer records a different time in Earth's history. For example, near the bottom is a dark rock called shale. It was once the muddy bottom of a shallow sea. Thin, pink layers of rock were fertile soils, and a layer of orange sandstone used to be a sandy river bottom. The Badlands' rocks show evidence of lakes, deserts, and volcanoes millions of years ago.

Over time, new sedimentary layers were deposited over older ones. The highest layer is the youngest, and the lowest layer is the oldest. The oldest visible layers in the Badlands formed about 75 million years ago!

Pinnacles are pointier than buttes. The different bands of color are layers of sedimentary rock.

4

BUTTES AND PINNACLES

Walking on, visitors bump into buttes and pinnacles. Shadows dance across a dramatic, steep-sided butte that towers over its surroundings. Buttes are the most common landform in the Badlands. How did these flat-topped columns form?

Rocks in the Badlands vary from soft to hard. The softer rocks are less resistant to weathering, so they erode faster. This is called **differential erosion,** meaning that hard rocks and soft rocks erode at different rates.

A butte in Badlands National Park

When a layer of harder rock is surrounded by softer rock, the softer rock erodes away much sooner than the harder rock. Eventually this can produce a butte. A butte is a raised, horizontal platform that looks like a giant stool.

Pinnacles, which are related to buttes, point upward like fingers. Buttes narrow into pinnacles as they erode at the edges.

GULLYWASHERS

Ridges as thin as a knife's edge line up against the sky. Sometimes dark storm clouds loom beyond the ridges. Minutes later a cool wind kicks up, followed by a clap of thunder and a burst of hard rain. Hikers move to higher ground.

It's a good opportunity to observe the processes that have shaped the Badlands. Rainwater gathers into small streams that are brown with silt. A backpack-sized piece of shale splashes down into a stream.

Here rains are infrequent but heavy, and downpours can wash soil and rock away in a hurry. No wonder they're nicknamed "gullywashers." They do "wash out" the gullies, which are narrow channels carved by flowing rainwater.

The storm passes quickly and the gullies soon dry up. Each time it rains, the landscape is slightly altered.

Anyone walking past a butte or pinnacle can expect to find hoodoos, too. Hoodoos

are pillars of softer rock capped by a flat "hat" of harder rock. The cap shields the rock directly below it from erosion, like a rock umbrella. Hoodoos are a good example of what differential erosion can do.

IN THE BLINK OF AN EYE

Altogether, weathering and erosion eat away about 2.5 centimeters (1 inch) of badlands rock every year. That adds up to almost 5 kilometers (3 miles) in 500,000 years. At this rate, the Badlands will have eroded away in another 500,000 years. Where rocks are concerned, that's in the blink of an eye. Hikers are lucky to experience this strange landscape at the height of its beauty. The landscape will look very different half a million years from now.

The vertical, sloping grooves are gullies. Some gullies are no bigger than wrinkles. Others are wider. Some might eventually grow into canyons.

NATURE'S SCULPTURE GARDENS

Native Americans and French explorers usually avoided the Badlands because traveling through it was difficult and dangerous. Today roads, maps, and clearly-marked trails make traveling easier. Tired, thirsty hikers can return to air-conditioned vehicles with a deeper appreciation of this marvel of nature.

There are other badlands in the world. Like Badlands National Park, all badlands seem like places on another planet. The South Dakota Badlands are one of the most famous in the world. They contain some of the weirdest and most wonderful rocks around.

Hiking through the Badlands can be like going on a scavenger hunt. What other outlandish land features might visitors discover here?

WORMHOLES Some sandstone rocks sport pencil-thin holes called wormholes. Most geologists think the holes were left by ancient roots, not worms.

Boo! It's a hoodoo. The top layer of rock is more resistant than the layers under it. The harder rock forms a "cap." The cap protects underlying rock from erosion.

WINDOWS Weathering and erosion formed this window in the Wall at Badlands National Park.

POPCORN When some clay-rich rocks get soaked, they dry into a bumpy, sticky surface called popcorn.

ARMORED MUD BALLS Flowing water rolls a piece of sticky clay mud into a ball. The mud ball rolls down a gully, picking up sand and pebbles. The pebbles form a layer of "armor" around the mud ball.

Check In What causes rocks in the Badlands to have unusual shapes?

A ROCK TOUR Through Time

by Beth Geiger

illustrations by Robert Hynes

These days, the Badlands are dry, dusty, and surrounded by a sun-scorched prairie, but it wasn't always like this. The colorful horizontal bands striping the cliffs are layers of **sedimentary rock.** The layers reveal long-lost worlds far different from what you see today.

The layers contain information about the past, which geologists have studied carefully. They've learned this place was once at the bottom of a warm ocean. Fast-forward to a few million years after that, and it was a lush, swampy forest. Bizarre animals swam and searched for food here. The Badlands' rocks even reveal the direction in which past rivers flowed, and in what direction the waves lapped an ancient shoreline. How can rocks reveal so much?

Sedimentary rocks in the Badlands offer so much information because they started out as soft layers of sediments, such as pebbles, sand, dust, mud, and shells. The kinds of sediment in these rocks give clues about the prehistoric environments that existed here. Ripple marks, sand dunes, and animal bones have also been preserved. Once the sediments were buried, pressure and chemical changes hardened them into sedimentary rock.

Layers are a characteristic of most sedimentary rocks. Newer layers build on top of older ones, so the oldest layers are at the bottom and the youngest ones are at the top. This is called the **law of superposition.** Let's use the law of superposition to travel back in time!

FOLLOW THOSE LAYERS!

A number of different environments existed here during different times. Now that you have the law of superposition in your time-traveler's toolbox, you're ready to start. Your "rock tour" begins with the oldest, lowest layer of exposed rock in the park. Good luck!

It's 75 million years ago, long before humans walked on Earth. The Pierre Shale, the oldest and lowest layer of exposed rock in the Badlands, is just being deposited. The Pierre Shale was named after the area where geologists first described it in Pierre, South Dakota.

You are swimming in a warm, salty sea, the Western Interior Seaway. Dinosaurs roam swamps and forests along the coasts. Sea turtles, fish, and toothy reptiles called mosasaurs, which can be more than 14 meters (46 feet) long, swim in the sea. Mosasaurs have double-hinged jaws, much like a snake's, so they can swallow large animals whole. On second thought, you might be better off dodging *Tyrannosaurus rex* on land.

As you swim frantically toward a distant shore, silt filters down through the seawater and settles on the bottom. Clams, ammonites, and microscopic hard-shelled plankton swim all around you. When these organisms die, their bodies also settle to the bottom, where their hard shells can last millions of years. The mud and tiny shells will one day form the Pierre Shale, which is mostly shale rock with some limestone.

The Pierre Shale formed in the Western Interior Seaway. It can be found as far south as New Mexico.

PIERRE SHALE: BURIED AT SEA

TYPE OF ROCK: Shale and some limestone

APPEARANCE: Dull black to dark gray to reddish in color

DEPOSITED: 69–75 million years ago

ENVIRONMENT: A warm, shallow, inland sea

COOL CLUES: Fossils of sea creatures such as ammonites prove this was once a sea floor.

An ammonite fossil

FUN FACT: Native Americans had a legend to explain the huge fossil bones of mosasaurs. The legend told of a sea monster who flooded Earth and then was turned to stone.

Today's Caspian Sea is a huge saltwater lake. The shallow, warm sea that covered the Badlands 75 million years ago may have looked similar.

Leap ahead to 65 million years ago, higher up in the Badlands rock layers. You're standing on some seriously big mudflats. What happened during the past ten million years?

The Rocky Mountains are forming thousands of kilometers west of here. This has caused the land between the Western Interior Seaway and the Rockies to tilt upward, pushing back the seaway. It's a little ways east of here. The black, mucky sea bottom is now mudflats that stretch on and on.

A little to the west, deep forests grow on a broad plain that slopes upward toward the Rockies. Rivers wind through these forests toward the shrinking seaway.

The dinosaurs and mosasaurs have become extinct. Scientists think they were wiped out by a huge asteroid hitting Earth. Even so, if you cross the sticky mudflats to the sea's edge and cast in a fishing net, you will probably catch something. Plenty of fish and other creatures still thrive here.

As forests grow on the mudflats, the mud develops into a thick layer of soil. Over time, contact with the air changes the color from black and gray to a bright, rusty orange. This ancient soil, called the Yellow Mounds, is an example of a paleosol, or **fossil** soil. It's easy to imagine it as soil, with its abundant root holes. The Yellow Mounds look like rounded, orange-to-yellow hills in the Badlands.

YELLOW MOUNDS: OLDER THAN DIRT

TYPE OF ROCK: Paleosol (fossil soil)

APPEARANCE: Orange to yellow; forms mounds or slopes

DEPOSITED: About 65 million years ago, right after the dinosaurs became extinct

ENVIRONMENT: Mudflats and forests

COOL CLUES: Clay-filled holes from tree roots show that big trees grew in this soil.

A view of the Yellow Mounds

FUN FACT: The Yellow Mounds may have started with a bang. A jumbled, crumpled layer called the Disturbed Zone lies between the Pierre Shale and the Yellow Mounds. It may be the result of an asteroid impact about 65 million years ago.

A mudflat in Alaska is exposed during low tide. Long before the Badlands was a badlands, it was a mudflat.

Forests and floods

Twenty-six million years have gone by. The last of the Western Interior Seaway disappeared nearly 15 million years ago. Rivers flow across a plain where the seaway used to be. Tropical forests cover the plain, and the air is warm and misty.

Alligators thrive in these swampy forests, and so do many new mammals. Some look familiar, but many will die out long before the present day. The first squirrels scamper around, along with pocket gophers, peccaries (pig-like mammals), and saber-toothed cats. All of them seem small compared to the *Titanotherium*, a horned mammal that looks like a cross between an elephant and a rhinoceros.

For now the climate is still hot and humid, but the land is slowly rising. This is causing the climate to become drier and cooler. Open meadows have begun to dot the forests.

One piece at a time, rivers are slowly eroding the Black Hills to the west. They spread the pebbles, sand, and silt particles across the forested floodplain. Sometimes the rivers flood and coat everything with a layer of fine silt. As the rivers empty into lakes, different-sized sediments settle to the bottom. They eventually form layers of conglomerate, a type of sedimentary rock with bits of large sediments. Geologists call the layers deposited during this time the Chadron Formation.

CHADRON: MONSTER MISHMASH

TYPE OF ROCK: Claystone, conglomerate, sandstone

APPEARANCE: Pale gray-green; erodes into rounded hills

DEPOSITED: 34–37 million years ago

ENVIRONMENT: Rivers, forests, and shallow lakes on a broad plain

COOL CLUES: The Chadron Formation contains sediments from the Black Hills to the west. It's a clue that rivers flowed generally east.

FUN FACT: So many *Titanotherium* fossils have been found in the Chadron that the formation was originally named the "*Titanotherium* beds."

Conglomerate

The Badlands were once a forested floodplain. They may have looked similar to this floodplain in Japan.

33 MILLION YEARS AGO
Savanna

What a difference four million years has made! It's much sunnier, but cooler. The tropical forest has been replaced by trees that can withstand a chillier, drier climate.

Here alligators have died off, but some animals, such as the *Hyaenodon*, have survived since your last visit. These wolf-like predators snack on herds of oreodonts, which are herbivores that look like a cross between a pig and a camel. Oreodonts graze on leaves and shoots, because true grasses have not yet developed. Turtles bask on the banks of ponds and rivers.

If you skip ahead another million years, you will see that many rivers have dried up except during occasional floods. Animals drink from spring-fed watering holes. This looks something like the modern-day African savanna. In about 32 million years, scientists will find a fantastic variety of fossils in the Brule Formation.

The Brule Formation is a layer-by-layer look at a changing environment. Conditions changed so dramatically during this last million-year span that scientists divide the formation into two separate parts. The older layers were deposited on a watery floodplain. The younger layers of the Brule Formation show a rapid change to a much drier environment.

BRULE: BATTLE OF THE BANDS

TYPE OF ROCK: Paleosols, sandstone, claystone

APPEARANCE: The most colorful rocks in the Badlands, with rusty red, grayish white, pink, and greenish bands of rock

DEPOSITED: 30–34 million years ago

ENVIRONMENT: Dry, open savanna and scattered woodlands

An exposed paleosol

COOL CLUES: Researchers traced the course of ancient rivers. How? They made maps of the Brule's narrow bands of sandstone. The sandstone formed where rivers flowed.

FUN FACT: The famous Big Pig Dig gave scientists a window into life at a watering hole. More than 8,000 fossils were discovered in a layer of the Brule Formation.

True grasses had not yet appeared 33 million years ago, but the scene may have looked similar to today's African savanna.

*K*aboom! Volcanic ash is falling from the sky. Enormous eruptions are taking place in what is now Wyoming and Nebraska. The eruptions are so explosive that the ash is carried here from more than 1,600 kilometers (994 miles) away.

These volcanic eruptions continue on-and-off for millions of years, dropping layers of ash across the region like a thick, gray quilt.

The region is as dry as a desert. You spot a rabbit-like creature called *Paleolagus* scurrying instead of hopping. And a desert-loving beaver, *Palaeocastor*, pokes its head out of a burrow for a look around.

You can't stay here for long and you wouldn't want to. Volcanic ash contains tiny shards of glass and rock. The ash will pile up 15 meters (49 feet) thick in places. Today it is a white layer of rock at the bottom of the Sharps Formation.

After the ash is deposited, rivers sometimes flood the land with sand and silt. Bits of ash mix with the other sediments that form the rock layers of the Sharps Formation. Toughened by the ash, its layers of sandstone resist **erosion.** The park's highest pinnacles are made up of the sandstone. Most of the steep ridge called the Wall is part of the Sharps Formation, too.

SHARPS: NOTHING DULL ABOUT IT

TYPE OF ROCK: Volcanic tuff, sandstone mixed with ash

APPEARANCE: Light-colored layers; bottom layer formed from solid ash

DEPOSITED: 23–30 million years ago

ENVIRONMENT: Desert

COOL CLUES: Paleosols in the Sharps Formation help reveal how dry the climate was. They contain evidence of roots from desert plants such as sagebrush.

FUN FACT: Ancient beavers dug corkscrew-shaped burrows. The burrows have been perfectly preserved by volcanic ash.

Tuff

What happened after the Sharps layers were deposited? Scientists don't know. The last 23 million years are a mystery. Any younger rocks that formed on top of the Sharps Formation have eroded away.

It's been a rock tour of rock bands. The law of superposition helped you travel back in time. But 500,000 years from now, erosion will have removed all of these rock layers. What will this place be like then? The future is anybody's guess.

The Badlands may once have resembled this volcanic desert in Argentina.

Check In | What can geologists learn about the past by studying sedimentary rock in the Badlands?

THE BIG

Subhyracodon

Archaeotherium

Mesohippus

Thirty-two million years ago, the Badlands of South Dakota were a broad, sweeping plain.

Low scrub and scattered trees grew on flat land beneath a pale sky. It rarely rained, so many thirsty animals flocked to a few muddy, spring-fed watering holes. The environment was similar to the present-day African savanna. But it was the wildlife, not the landscape, that was strange.

Some wildlife were relatives of today's animals. An early version of a horse stood only as tall as a large dog. The *Archaeotherium* looked like a long-jawed pig, but was as big as a cow. Herds of herbivores called oreodonts roamed the savanna like modern sheep. Miniature deer grew just 30 centimeters (12 inches) tall. Hornless rhinoceroses called *Subhyracodon* wallowed in mud holes. Wolf-sized *Hyaenodon* preyed on them all.

PIG DIG

by Beth Geiger   illustrations by Bob Kayganich

Oreodonts

Hyaenodon

Stuck in the mud

It's a typical day on the ancient savanna. Groups of thirsty animals gather at a shallow watering hole. Clumps of tall, grass-like plants grow on the muddy banks. A *Subhyracodon* is stuck in the mud and cannot free itself. As it bellows in frustration, the other animals sense danger and move away. Seconds later, a *Hyaenodon* leaps onto the *Subhyracodon's* back. Its powerful jaws clamp down with a dreadful crunch!

Hundreds of animals like the *Subhyracodon* died here. Their bones were either destroyed or buried in the soft ground. Over millions of years, chemical changes turned some of the buried bones into **fossils.**

The discovery of these fossils gave badlands **paleontologists** their biggest break ever. A paleontologist is a scientist who studies prehistoric life. This discovery became known as the Big Pig Dig.

OLIGOCENE PARK

A paleontology student uses a dental pick at the Big Pig Dig.

A lucky find In June 1993, visitors to Badlands National Park discovered a backbone sticking out of the ground. In the Badlands, rapid **erosion** exposes fossils fairly often. But this backbone was unusually large and well preserved. At first, scientists thought the bones were from an *Archaeotherium,* which looked like a big pig. They learned later the fossil was from a hornless rhino, but the name "Big Pig Dig" stuck.

Scientists estimated they only needed four days to excavate the fossils at the Big Pig Dig, but they kept finding more fossils. The site had so many fossils that paleontologists from the South Dakota School of Mines and Technology spent 15 summers there. Meanwhile, the Big Pig Dig became a top attraction for thousands of visitors each year. By 2008, more than 10,000 bones had been identified.

Paleontologists developed a picture of the scene from 33 million years ago. The bones were from a period called the Oligocene Epoch, when mammals ruled

Tools of the Trade

How do paleontologists uncover fossils? They dig slowly and carefully. They use tools that can free delicate fossils from surrounding rock without damaging the fossils.

ᐱ Dental picks are great tools for jobs that require precision. With dental picks, paleontologists can chip away rock from the tiniest parts of a fossil.

❯ Soft brushes remove loose soil and rock without scraping or scratching fossils. Once fossils are brought to a lab, paleontologists can use air brushes, which blow a jet of air, to finish the job.

❮ Trowels are terrific for exposing fossils in soft material such as clay.

Earth. Paleontologists discovered the bones of at least 18 types of mammals at this ancient watering hole. They found no dinosaur bones because the dinosaurs had died out about 32 million years earlier. If Badlands National Park contains dinosaur bones, they are in much deeper, older layers of rock.

Digging for fossils is exciting, but it is also a slow, painstaking process that can take a long time to complete.

Paleontologists must take care not to break the fossils and destroy important clues. Most fossils are extremely fragile, so paleontologists use tiny tools to free fossils from rock. Then they carefully record, label, and pack each specimen for transport. This is hot and dusty work under the blazing South Dakota sun.

For each hour of fieldwork, paleontologists can spend another 12 hours in the laboratory repairing and studying every fossil they discovered.

People often don't realize that a fossil can be any preserved evidence of ancient life, not just bones.

Animal tracks, petrified wood, leaf impressions, and animal droppings can all be fossils. Fossils can be as big as an elephant or as tiny as a microscopic organism.

How did Badlands paleontologists re-create the scene at the Big Pig Dig? Taphonomy is the branch of paleontology that investigates questions that can help fill in the gaps. For example, how did the animal die? Where was it, and what was it doing? Like detectives, taphonomists look for clues in the position and condition of fossils to figure out what happened.

Larger fossils must be protected for transport to the lab. Paleontologists wrap the fossils in a plaster jacket, or cast. They mix up a batch of plaster and pour it over the fossil. The plaster hardens into a protective covering that is removed at the lab.

Paleontologists work with geologists, biologists, and other scientists to understand the evidence fully.

Paleo-puzzle pieces

After 15 summers studying 10,000 specimens, scientists think the site was a watering hole where animals gathered to drink. Some animals became prey. Others were stranded in the sticky mud.

Paleontologists reached this conclusion by analyzing thousands of fossils and sorting them into individual animals. It was like a bony jigsaw puzzle that took about 15 years to put together!

Many crushed bones were a clue that this was once a busy watering hole. "The bones showed evidence of trampling," says paleontologist Rachel Benton. Fossils also were found scattered in every direction. That clue told researchers the animals hadn't died in a river. Otherwise, currents might have caused the bones to rest in a similar position and direction.

The soft parts of animals usually decay before they become fossilized. Hard parts, such as bones and teeth, are tougher. Teeth are especially tough. Teeth are also small. They are less likely to get broken than bigger bones.

Check In   What was unusual or significant about the Big Pig Dig?

Fossil Phil

by Beth Geiger

On airplane flights, Phil Manning hopes for a prehistoric seatmate, ideally a dinosaur. Phil often gets his wish, since he carries dinosaur **fossils** from the field to the American Museum of Natural History in New York. Each summer Phil travels from England to South Dakota. There he digs for animals that lived during the Cretaceous Period over 65 million years ago.

Phil lives for the science, adventure, and excitement of being a **paleontologist.** He tells us about his life as a dinosaur hunter.

NATIONAL GEOGRAPHIC: How did you get interested in paleontology?

PHIL MANNING: When I was five years old my parents took me to the Natural History Museum in London, where I first saw dinosaurs. I was hooked! I started

PHILLIP MANNING is a paleontologist. He excavates and studies fossils of dinosaurs and other extinct creatures. This helps him explore what life was like tens of millions of years ago. Dr. Manning analyzes the fossils in his laboratory. He hopes to find out what these creatures looked like, how they moved, and even the colors of their skin.

collecting fossil shells in my backyard. When I was seven I discovered my first fossil bone. It was a marine reptile over 180 million years old. I still have this fossil bone today. It was much later in school when I discovered that paleontology could be a real career. I still pinch myself on a regular basis to check that I am not dreaming.

NG: Do you have a "favorite fossil ever" or most exciting find?

PHIL MANNING: Almost every fossil I find is precious. Possibly the most important fossil ever discovered was the one that started people wanting to learn more about the history of life. However, if I was pushed to answer, my favorite fossil is the one that we have not yet discovered. I think there is always something out there that will advance our knowledge and understanding of life on Earth.

Phil Manning in South Dakota's badlands

NATIONAL GEOGRAPHIC: What's your fieldwork like?

PHIL MANNING: I spend as much time as I can in a 65 million-year-old layer of rock in South Dakota called the Hell Creek Formation. There, my team and I dig up plenty of gorgeous dinosaur bones. We also get sunburned, try to avoid the local rattlesnakes, and often get eaten alive by mosquitoes. But I would not exchange this for anything!

Once a fossil is carefully uncovered, we apply a plaster "jacket" to protect the bone on its journey back to the museum in New York. We excavate, plaster, and transport over a ton of fossil bones every summer. It's exhausting work, but hugely satisfying for all involved. The fieldwork relies upon the energy and enthusiasm of a large team of folks. They all work very hard each summer to learn more about the dinosaurs, plants, and other animals whose fossil remains we excavate from the Hell Creek sediments.

NG: What do you do when you aren't in the field?

PHIL MANNING: I teach several courses convincing college students that paleontology rocks! I also try to find time to study fossils in the lab.

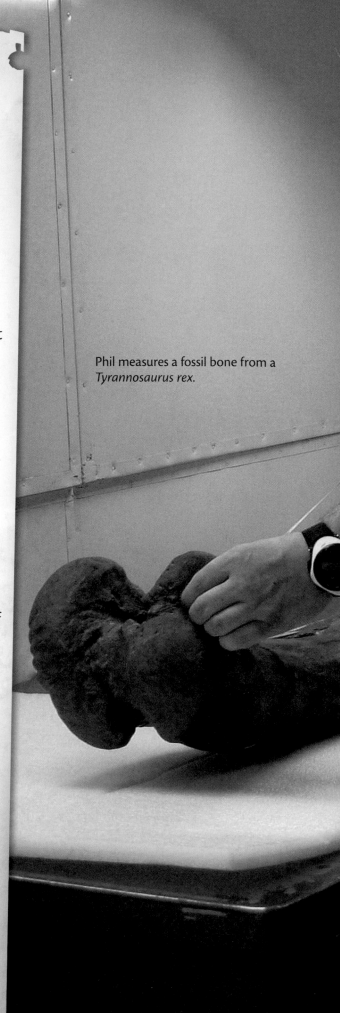

Phil measures a fossil bone from a *Tyrannosaurus rex*.

My team and I often use the latest technology to help us unlock the innermost secrets hidden in fossils. We even find time to work with powerful X-ray machines that help determine the skin color and patterns of long-extinct animals. Our team eventually hopes to discover the full skin-color range of past life. We are still working on that!

NG: How does paleontology apply to the modern world?

PHIL MANNING: The fossil record provides insight into processes and patterns of life, like climate change and extinction events. It can help us better understand similar events impacting life on Earth today. The past has the potential to be a key to unlock our understanding of the future.

NG: What questions do you hope to answer in your future work?

PHIL MANNING: The work we are currently doing, on how fossils are preserved through deep time, is some of the most exciting work I have been involved in during my whole career. We are beginning to understand the chemical pathways that give rise to fossils. My team and I also want to explore and answer new questions that have not been asked before, as this is where the real excitement in science often lies.

Check In What information can paleontologists learn from fossils?

Discuss

1. Explain how you think the four pieces in *The Disappearing Badlands* are connected.

2. What do you think are the connections between this book's title and the unusual landforms in "Gullies, Buttes, and Hoodoos"?

3. Choose one of the sedimentary layers named in "A Rock Tour Through Time." Use information in the text to explain why it provides a good model of how some sedimentary rock forms.

4. Explain how scientists at the Big Pig Dig studied the fossils to learn about the past environment. Compare and contrast their methods with Phil Manning's.

5. What questions do you still have about the Badlands or paleontology? What would be some good ways to find out more?